Darius, Artaxerxes, and Ahasuerus in the Bible

James B. Jordan

Athanasius Press
205 Roselawn
Monroe, Louisiana 71201
http://www. athanasiuspress.org

Darius, Artaxerxes, and Ahasuerus in the Bible
© 2014 by James B. Jordan
All rights reserved.

ISBN: 978-0-9842439-5-2 (softcover)

Table of Contents

Introduction 5

---

1 The Jewish Use of Names . . . 9

2 The Names of the Persian Kings . . 17

3 Genealogical Evidence in Ezra and Nehemiah . 25

4 The Persian Kings in Ezra 4–6 . . 41

5 The Setting of the Book of Esther . . 49

6 The Seventy "Weeks" of Daniel 9:24–27 . 65

Chronological Appendix . . . 69

Introduction

The thesis of this study is that the Persian kings named Darius, Ahasuerus, and Artaxerxes in the books of Ezra, Nehemiah, and Esther are one and the same. This is not a new understanding, but an examination of recent commentaries on these books shows that this possibility is not even entertained, so certain are these expositors that "Ahasuerus" is the king the Greeks called Xerxes and that "Artaxerxes" is Artaxerxes Longimanus.[1] I hope to show, however, that the common identifications of these kings is problematic and that understanding their common identity sheds considerable light on the nature of the texts under consideration.

The reader should understand at the outset that there are two general traditions about this matter. On the one hand is the tradition found in most Bible commentaries, which is that the

---

1. For instance, Jacob M. Meyers, *Ezra-Nehemiah*, Anchor Bible 14 (Garden City, NY: Doubleday, 1965); Derek Kidner, *Ezra and Nehemiah*, Tyndale Old Testament Commentaries (Leicester, England: Inter-Varsity Press, 1979); F. Charles Fensham, *The Books of Ezra and Nehemiah*, New International Commentary on the Old Testament (Grand Rapids: Eerdmans, 1982); H. G. M. Williamson, *Ezra, Nehemiah,* Word Biblical Commentary 16 (Waco, TX: Word, 1985).

Artaxerxes of Ezra 7ff. and Nehemiah is Longimanus. On the other hand is the tradition found in most Bible chronologers, which is that Artaxerxes is another name for Darius. In general, the difference can be accounted for by the fact that chronologists tend to build more on genealogical data, while expositors and commentators are generally more interested in either text-critical matters or theological teachings. As regards the book of Esther, there was considerable diversity of opinion until the late nineteenth century, when it was established to the satisfaction of the scholarly community that "Ahasuerus" is the Hebrew form of "Xerxes."

This study is not offered as a certain proof. Rather, the argument is that identifying Ahasuerus and Artaxerxes with Darius provides a simpler explanation when all the data are taken into account. My argument is just a form of Occam's Razor, that the simpler explanation is to be preferred.

The reader should also understand that there are two groups of scholars that are not really open to my thesis. The first consists of Seventh-Day Adventists, many of whom, especially William H. Shea, have done much worthwhile work on the details of ancient Babylonian and Persian history. Seventh-Day Adventists, however, believe that Ellen G. White was a prophet and thus are largely bound to her views. White prophetically stated that the 2300 evenings and mornings of Daniel 8:14 were not days but represented years and that they ended in AD 1843. This means that they began in 457 BC. which was also affirmed to be the beginning of the seventy "weeks" of years of Daniel 9:25. This date is linked to the decree of "Artaxerxes" in Ezra 7. Thus, Seventh-Day Adventist scholars are religiously committed to seeing the Artaxerxes of Ezra-Nehemiah as Longimanus.

The second group consists of evangelical fundamentalist scholars, who believe in a "literal wherever possible" hermeneutic and thus are committed up front to believing that Daniel's 70 "weeks" of years must be taken literally. Dispensational fundamentalists believe that the first 69 "weeks" terminate at the cross and resurrection of Jesus. Non-dispensational fundamentalists are open to the possibility that Jesus' death is predicted for the middle of the 70th "week." Some hold to an AD 30 date for the crucifixion of Jesus, and some to an AD 33 date. Whatever the case, the fundamentalist is required to count literally backwards from either date to find a decree in the reign of Longimanus. Thus, because of their hermeneutical commitments, fundamentalist scholars will seldom be open to the thesis of this monograph.

Other evangelical and conservative Christian scholars, however, are open to the possibility that Daniel's 70 "weeks" of years is a symbol of the time from Cyrus's decree to the cross, which in chapter 6 of this monograph I shall argue is the case. Such conservatives have no reason not to entertain the interpretative approach offered here. The same is true for non-evangelical scholars of various sorts.

If my thesis is correct, then several things emerge. First, it becomes clear that there was no "decree to rebuild Jerusalem" issued by Artaxerxes Longimanus, because that later Artaxerxes is not the Artaxerxes (Darius) of Nehemiah. Thus, the "word" spoken of in Daniel 9:25 must be the decree of Cyrus.

Second, it becomes clear that, just as Cyrus was a new David, so Darius is a new Solomon. It is Darius who builds the Temple, Darius-Artaxerxes who builds Jerusalem, and Darius-Ahasuerus who marries a Jewish bride and protects the Jewish people, which creates a broad analogy between the books of Esther and Song of Solomon.

Third, assuming for a moment that Chronicles-Ezra-Nehemiah were designed as one book with one story, then the plan of that large book becomes clear: the progression from David to Solomon to his wayward successors is rehearsed as a typological foundation for the new historical progression from Cyrus to Darius to their wayward successors in both empire and land.

Of course, none of these Biblico-theological considerations is sound if my thesis is incorrect. The thesis must be defended, and then the Biblico-theological reflections can begin in earnest.

It is not my purpose to provide an extensive discussion of who has written what on this subject. To do so would be to extend the length of this monograph considerably: a dissertation could be written on the history of interpretation of the several matters within the scope of this monograph. Since twentieth-century expositors have ignored this possibility, there is virtually no contemporary literature on the subject to take up and interact with.

Some, though not all, of the arguments in chapter 3 of this monograph are taken from Martin Anstey, *The Romance of Bible Chronology*, originally published in 1913 and occasionally reprinted. This is an uneven work, but many of its arguments are well worth considering on a host of issues related to its subject matter. I have updated, corrected, and filled out some of Anstey's arguments and have presented others of my own.

One
The Jewish Use of Names

To begin with, let us list the relevant Persian kings, using the names the Greeks used for them, which are the names everyone uses for them today:

539–530 BC	Cyrus
530–522 BC	Cambyses II
522–487 BC	Darius I
487–466 BC	Xerxes I
465–425 BC	Artaxerxes Longimanus[1]

The Greek historians of the ancient world used the names Darius, Xerxes (Ahasuerus),[2] and Artaxerxes as names, pure and

---

1. Various dictionaries, encyclopaedias, and commentaries give slightly varying dates for these kings, shifting the dates forward or backward one year. The dates used here are from the Chronological Appendix of this monograph.

2. On the equivalence of "Xerxes" and "Ahasuerus," see chapter 2 of the present study.

Darius, Artaxerxes, and Ahasuerus in the Bible

simple. They seem to have assumed that each of these kings used only one of these names to designate himself.

The Jewish writers, who after all lived in Persia and were closer to the Persian culture, used these names more fluidly. In the apocryphal Additions to Esther, the king is called not Ahasuerus (Xerxes) but Artaxerxes. The Greek version of the Hebrew Scriptures prepared by the Jews living in Alexandria calls him Artaxerxes throughout the translation of Esther.

The apocryphal book of 1 Esdras, chapter 3, begins by describing a feast of Darius using the very language used for the feast of Ahasuerus (Xerxes) in Esther chapter 1. Whoever wrote this book seems to have assumed that Esther's king was in fact Darius.

Josephus calls the Artaxerxes of Ezra 7 by the name Xerxes, though he sees this Xerxes as the successor to Darius.[3] He sees Esther's king as Artaxerxes Longimanus.[4] Thus, Josephus reverses the order of these kings as they are commonly understood today.

The Jewish book *Seder Olam*, a product of the early Babylonian talmudic scholars in the AD 200s, identifies both the Ahasuerus of Esther and the Artaxerxes of Ezra-Nehemiah as Darius. It begins its retelling of the story of Esther, "In the third year of his reign," immediately after "work at the Temple in Jerusalem stopped and was idle until year two of Darius the King"; thus, "his reign"—the reign of Esther's king—is that of Darius. And it states that Ezra came to Jerusalem the next year after the completion of the Temple in the reign of Darius.[5]

Now, these various extra-Biblical Jewish writings were written much later than the books of Ezra-Nehemiah and Esther.

---

3. Josephus, *Antiquities* 11:5:1.
4. Ibid., 11:6:1.
5. *Seder Olam: The Rabbinic View of Biblical Chronology*, trans. Henrich W. Guggenheimer (Northvale, NJ: Jason Aronson, 1998), 247–52.

The Jewish Use of Names

They conflict with one another and show other signs of confusion. They were written after contact with the Greek historians. But contrasting them provides something interesting. Josephus, who was pretty thoroughly Hellenized and quite at home with the Greek traditions, assumes that Darius, Xerxes, and Artaxerxes as found in the Bible were three different kings, even though he reverses Xerxes and Artaxerxes. The Babylonian scholars, though writing a couple of centuries later, assume that all three names apply to Darius. These scholars were closer to the historical-geographical context of these events, since they lived in the lands where they took place, and possibly preserved more accurate information.

Regardless of whether these Jewish writers were right or not, what they show us is that they were quite willing to give different names to these Persian kings, names at variance with the sacred text that they regarded to be Divinely inspired. They could not have engaged in this practice unless they assumed that a given king might be called by more than one name. For one thing, these writers would not have dared to tamper with the information found in the sacred text. For another, once their writings were issued to the Jewish community, the community would cry out against them unless the community also assumed that a given king might be called by more than one name.

We don't see these writers confusing David and Solomon and Rehoboam, for instance. It would not have occurred to them to switch their names around, because they knew that each man had one name. The fact that they were willing to switch around the names of the Persian kings shows that they assumed it was unproblematic to do so and that the Jewish community within which they wrote also assumed this.

How was this seeming confusion possible? In chapter 2 of this monograph we shall see that the name Darius means something like "Upholder of the Good," the name Ahasuerus

(Xerxes) means something like "Chief/Hero Among Kings," and the name Artaxerxes means "Kingdom of Justice." These are not personal names, but titles, or "throne-names." In this chapter we are interested in how the Jews used these names. Even if the Persians never used any other name for a given king, the possibility exists that the Jews used the names differently. Since these are throne-names, the Jews might have used them that way, just as they called all the Egyptian kings "Pharaoh."

Since we are interested in the Biblical literature and how the scribes who wrote Esther and Ezra-Nehemiah might have used these names, let us look at the Biblical use of names.

First of all, the names of foreign kings are very often omitted, and only titles or throne-names are used. I have mentioned Pharaoh, a throne-name meaning "Great House." Rarely does the Bible add the particular name of a Pharaoh, as in the case of Necho (2 Chron. 35–36). The same is true as regards the kings of Syria, who are all called Ben-Hadad ("Son of [the god] Hadad"; Jeremiah 49:27; Amos 1:4). We also see this in the case of the early Philistine kings, who are called Abimelech ("My Father is King; My Father is Melech"; Genesis 20, 26. Notice that in the title of Psalm 34, the Philistine king Achish is called Abimelech.).

The Biblical writers did not always do this. The kings of Babylon are called by their personal names. But these are personal names, while Darius, Xerxes, and Artaxerxes are throne-names or titles.

The second thing to bear in mind is that Biblical writers often use names significantly, according to their meaning. Everyone knows that names like Abram ("Mighty Father"), Isaac ("Laughter"), Jacob ("Replacement"), Israel ("God's Wrestler"), and many others are intimately connected to events in their lives. To take another familiar example, the name Melchizedek, king of Salem (Gen. 14:18–20), is explained and exegeted by the author of Hebrews: "First of all, by translation [of 'melchizedek']

The Jewish Use of Names

King of Righteousness, and then also King of Salem, which means King of Peace" (Heb. 7:2).

The use of various names on different occasions would be for literary and theological reasons. This is why the Bible sometimes calls the deity "God" (*'elohim*), "LORD" (*yahweh*), "Lord" (*'adonai*), and so forth. Recall also the variation between "Jacob" and "Israel" in the text of Genesis and elsewhere, when referring to the same individual.

Closer to the era of Ezra-Nehemiah and Esther is the book of Daniel. There Daniel is also called Belteshazzar, and his three friends Hananiah, Mishael, and Azariah are also called Shadrach, Meshach, and Abed-nego. The strong weight of evidence now favors taking Darius the Mede as another name for Cyrus the Persian.[6] The variation in the use of these names in Daniel is for theological reasons.

The use of two names for the same king can be seen elsewhere, even within the space of a few verses, as when an Assyrian king is called Pul in 2 Kings 15:19 and Tiglath-Pileser only a few verses later (v. 29). The Israelite king called Uzziah ("Yah is My Strength") by Isaiah and the Chronicler is called Azariah ("Yah has Helped") in 2 Kings 15. Saul's son Ishbaal ("Man of the Lord") is called Ishbosheth ("Man of Shame") in some places, clearly for theological reasons (1 Chron. 8:33; 2 Sam. 2:8).

Ezra 6:22 is a significant example of the theological character of Jewish writing as it pertains to how kings were designated. There we read that the Jews rejoiced because God "had turned the heart of the king of Assyria toward them." This king is Darius

---

6. See James M. Bulman, "The Identification of Darius the Mede," *Westminster Theological Journal* 35 (1973), 247–67; Brian E. Colless, "Cyrus the Persian as Darius the Mede in the Book of Daniel," *Journal for the Study of the Old Testament* 56 (1992), 113–26; and the other studies cited in these two articles.

Darius, Artaxerxes, and Ahasuerus in the Bible

king of Persia. Here he is called the king of Assyria, an empire long dead. The presence of this phrase in the text is not the result of a copyist's error. Rather, the reason is to remind the reader that the exile began when the northern part of the nation of Israel was taken into Assyrian captivity. That captivity was intensified when southern Israel (Judah) was taken into Babylonian captivity. The captivity began to be over when the Jews returned from Babylon in the second year of Cyrus. Now the captivity is fully over as they return from the king "of Assyria."

Thus, in Ezra 6:22 what is "literally" erroneous (king of Assyria) is theologically correct. The writer can do this because he has already fully established that Darius of Persia is the king. Now he is able to add a theological nuance to what Darius has done by calling him the king of Assyria (which in a sense he was, since the Persian empire included Assyria).

This monograph argues that the writer has done exactly the same thing when he shifts from "Darius" to "Artaxerxes" in Ezra 7. I am arguing that the genealogical information in Ezra-Nehemiah establishes that the king throughout is Darius and that the writer begins to call him Artaxerxes in Ezra 7 for thematic or theological reasons, just as in 6:22 he calls him the king of Assyria.

So, let us consider the possible scenario. The writers of Esther and of Ezra-Nehemiah are writing theological works. They have a heritage of using throne-names for foreign kings and also of using names significantly. They consider that the names Ahasuerus (Xerxes) and Artaxerxes are titles or throne-names, and as such, from their point of view, these names might be used for more than one Persian king. Thus, these writers have open to them the possibility of selecting either one of these names to use for any given king, in order to make a theological point.

In other words, the possibility exists that, when the author of Esther calls his king Xerxes (Ahasuerus), he does not intend by this to tell us who this particular monarch was. Instead, he is calling him Ahasuerus (Xerxes) for a theological reason, for a reason connected to the theme of his book.

Let us assume for the moment that this is what he did. If so, we don't know from his name who this king was. He might have been Cambyses II, Darius, Xerxes I, or Artaxerxes Longimanus. To determine which king Ahasuerus was, we would have to look at other evidence.

If the name means "Chief Among Kings" or "Greatest of Kings," then the use of this title instead of the name Darius or Cambyses is part of the theological message of the book of Esther. We see in Esther that the king is pictured very much like Yahweh, living in a palace described much like the Temple and enthroned in a "holy of holies" that it is death to enter without permission. He is Yahweh's representative, God's present ruler on the earth. The Jews must interact with him on that basis, obeying his commands but witnessing God's truth to him. Thus, "Greatest of Kings" is an appropriate name for the ruler in the book of Esther, but it does not tell us who this particular king might have been.

Similarly, in Ezra-Nehemiah we find that Darius orders that the Temple be built. His throne-name means "Upholder of Good Deeds" and is appropriate to denote him as the one who orders the Temple to be built. It is built in the 6th year of Darius, and then immediately in the 7th year of "Artaxerxes" we find Ezra going to Jerusalem (Ezra 6–7). We have seen that it is entirely possible that the Jewish writer of Ezra-Nehemiah might change the name he uses for this king for theological reasons. What might that reason be? Well, having built the Temple, Darius has done just what was needed to establish his realm as a "Kingdom of Justice." Moreover, since the Temple is a house of prayer, building it does not completely establish Judea as a *realm* within his kingdom. Attention shifts in Ezra 7 to the matter of establishing the *society* in Jerusalem and Judea, which is of concern to one whose name is now "Kingdom of Justice."

Now as we conclude this chapter, it is important to emphasize that nothing is proven. We have only seen that it is entirely possible for the Jewish writers of these books to have used the throne-names of the Persian kings fluidly, for theological reasons. This does not mean that they in fact did so. And even if they did, we have not yet looked at any evidence that might show which king was the king in Esther and in the second half of Ezra and Nehemiah.

What I have sought to establish is that it would be simplistic to assume that the Jewish writers used these names the same way the Greek writers did and the same way the Persians did. We must interpret Jewish writings, and especially the Biblical writings, on their own terms. When we do so, we find that it is entirely possible that older writers, like Archbishop Ussher in his vast study of the history of the ancient world, were right in identifying both Ahasuerus and Artaxerxes with Darius.

Two
The Names of the Persian Kings

Though we know little about the Persian empire, culture, and history, the chronology of the early emperors seems fairly well-established. Cyrus was succeeded by his son Cambyses II in 530 BC, who reigned for seven and a half years. Cambyses II had apparently put his brother Smerdis to death in order to secure the throne, but upon Cambyses II's death, a certain "Smerdis" claimed the throne. Evidently this Pseudo-Smerdis was a Magian priest named Gomates or Gaumata. He reigned for half a year before being deposed by Darius I.

Darius reigned 36 years (522–487 BC) and was followed by Xerxes I, who reigned for 21 years (486–466 BC). He was followed by Artaxerxes Longimanus ("the Long-Handed"), who reigned for 40 years (465–425 BC). His successors, according to secular sources, were Darius II, Artaxerxes II, Artaxerxes III, Arogus, and Darius III.

Recent expositors of Ezra and Nehemiah take it that Haggai, Zechariah, Jeshua, and Zerubbabel rebuilt the temple and altar in the early years of Darius I's reign, as recorded in Ezra 1–6. This

Darius, Artaxerxes, and Ahasuerus in the Bible

carries us down to 516 BC, the 6th year of Darius. Then we skip 57 years down to 459 BC, the 7th year of Artaxerxes Longimanus (Ezra 7:1, 8). The events of Nehemiah take us down to at least the 33rd year of Artaxerxes (Neh. 13:6), 433 BC.

Bible chronologists such as Ussher, Lightfoot, Anstey, and Faulstich and some of the older commentators (like John Gill) have criticized this approach. After all, it looks a bit suspicious to move from the 6th year of Darius to the 7th of Artaxerxes Longimanus (Ezra 6–7), and this invites inquiry.

The Meanings of the Names

These three names are throne-names, which the king took when he acceded to the throne. This is certain in the cases of "Xerxes" and "Artaxerxes" and almost certain in the case of "Darius." It used to be thought that Xerxes means "king" and Artaxerxes means "high king." This is based on a statement in Herodotus, "In Greek, the name Darius means the Doer, Xerxes means the Warrior, and Artaxerxes means the Great Warrior."[1]

This does not seem to be completely the case, however. The Persian for Artaxerxes is *Arta-khshasa*. *Arta* means "justice," and *khshasa* means "kingship, kingdom." The transposition of this name, "Kingdom of Justice,"[2] into Greek and Hebrew is as follows:

Persian:	Arta-khshasa
Greek:	Artaxerxes (Arta-ksherkshes)
Hebrew:	Artakhshast'

---

1. Herodotus, *The History* 6:98, trans. David Grene (Chicago: University of Chicago, 1987), 448.
2. J. M. Cook, *The Persian Empire* (New York: Schocken, 1983), 45.

The Names of the Persian Kings

The Persian for Xerxes is *Khshayarsha*. *Khshay* means "rule." J. M. Cook says that Xerxes perhaps means "hero among kings."[3] According to Carey Moore, Ahasuerus means "chief of rulers."[4] The transposition is as follows:

Persian:	Khshayarsha
Greek:	Xerxes (Khsherkhshes)
Hebrew:	'Akhashwerush

As can be seen, the Hebrew equivalent does not look a great deal like the Persian original. In the nineteenth century, however, trilingual inscriptions were uncovered that give the name Khshayarsha in Babylonian equivalents, and in clay tablets other Babylonian spellings were found, such as Akhshiyarshu, Akhshiyawarshu, etc.[5] The similarity of the Hebrew to the Babylonian is clearer, and the scholarly consensus is now that Ahasuerus is the same word as Khshayarsha and Xerxes.

Darius (Persian *Dareyavesh*) means "he who holds firm the good."[6] Others give something like "he who enjoys good things."[7] Given these meanings, it is likely that Darius is also a throne-name.

It is interesting that after Darius I, we only find these three "names" used by the Persian kings. Thus, we may suppose that each king as he came to the throne picked one of these three throne-names as the name he would use as ruler.

---

3. Idem.
4. *Esther*, Anchor Bible 7B (Garden City: Doubleday, 1971), 3.
5. Lewis Bayles Paton, *A Critical and Exegetical Commentary on the Book of Esther*, International Critical Commentary (Edinburgh: T. & T. Clark, 1908), 53f.
6. Idem.
7. Richard Frye, *The Heritage of Persia* (New York: World, 1963), 92.

In summary:

Darius =	Doer or Upholder of the Good
Xerxes/Ahasuerus =	Hero Among Kings;
	Greatest of Kings;
	Chief of Rulers
Artaxerxes =	Kingdom of Justice

The thesis of this monograph would be strengthened if there were evidence that some of the Persian kings used more than one of these throne-names for himself, but no such evidence has been discovered. We have little evidence from ancient Persia, but what we have gives no indication that Darius ever also called himself Xerxes or Artaxerxes, or that any other Persian king used more than one throne-name. It may be that they did so, but there is no evidence of it.[8]

All the same, since the Jewish scriptures call a given person by more than one name in order to make theological points, we cannot assume that the texts of Ezra-Nehemiah and Esther employ these name-titles in exactly the same way the Persian inscriptions do.

Evidence from Daniel

The fact that the book of Daniel refers to one and the same king as both Cyrus and Darius shows that Jewish writers could use different names for the same king in the same document. In Daniel 9:1 we have another striking piece of evidence that is

---

[8]. The reader is cautioned that on page 262 of Martin Anstey's *Romance of Bible Chronology*, an inscription of Xerxes is quoted in the course of which Xerxes calls himself Darius. This, however, is a mistranslation that led Anstey astray. A correct translation of this text (*XPa*) can be found at http://www.livius.org/aa-ac/achaemenians/XPa.html

The inscription of Artaxerxes Longimanus called *A1Pa* can be found on-line at http://www.livius.org/aa-ac/achaemenians/A1Pa.html

The Names of the Persian Kings

germane to our study: "In the first year of Darius the son of Ahasuerus from the seed of the Medes."

It is the use of "Ahasuerus" that interests us. Cyrus's father was named Cambyses (Cambyses I), and he was king of a small nation called Anshan, a Persian vassal state of Media. Cambyses I married Mandane, daughter of the Median king Astyages, and Cyrus was their son. The father of Astyages was Cyaxeres.

Now, which of these three men, if any, is intended by the name "Ahasuerus"? It is clear that none of them was named Khshayarsha (Xerxes). Some liberal commentators on Daniel have supposed that this statement is just a mistake and that Xerxes I is in view. It should be clear, however, that the supposedly-later author of Daniel and its audience were not so ignorant as to have made or accepted such an obvious error.

Goldingay suggests that it is Cyaxeres. Once again, we have to go beyond the Greek "Cyraxeres" to a Median or Akkadian original: "Uwakhshtra" (Median), "U-ak-sa-tar" or "Umakishtar" (Akkadian). The argument is that the Hebrew "Ahasuerus" is close to this (though not very close, it seems to me) and could arise from it just as it arose from the other name Khshayarsha.[9] In the apocryphal book Tobit (14:15), Cyaxeres is called Ahasuerus. Since there is no way to get from "Cambyses" or "Astyages" to "Ahasuerus," Cyaxeres would seem to be the only possibility.

I submit that this is a strained and unhelpful suggestion. It assumes that two different names have come into Hebrew as the same name. It is far simpler to assume that Ahasuerus (Xerxes) is a throne-name and was used by one or more of the kings in

---

9. John Goldingay, *Daniel*, Word Biblical Commentary 30 (Dallas: Word, 1989), 239. Goldingay provides a bibliography of other scholars who have made this suggestion.

Cyrus's ancestry, in which case there is no reason to try and figure out how "Cyaxeres" or "Astyages" could become "Ahasuerus." "Chief of Rulers" seems to make more sense as a title for Astyages or Cyaxeres than for Cambyses I of Anshan, but on the Cyrus Cylinder, Cambyses I is called "the great king, king of Anshan." Since this inscription is in Akkadian, not Persian, we don't know whether "great king" might be the full equivalent of Khshayarsha (Xerxes, Ahasuerus) or not. It is certainly similarly, if not fully equivalent, and close enough for Daniel's purposes: if Cambyses I had been called "great king," Daniel could easily use "Ahasuerus" as the equivalent.

Either of the other two kings might also have been called Xerxes (Ahasuerus) as a title. Yet, since Daniel 9:1 says, "son of Ahasuerus, of the seed of the Medes," it may be best to understand the text as saying that Cyrus was the son of his father Ahasuerus, Cambyses I, and of the seed of the Medes through his mother Mandane. (Compare the Hebrew usage of seed in Genesis 3:15, "seed of the woman.")

Since Daniel himself was the author of Daniel 9, he could not have picked up the throne-name Xerxes (Ahasuerus) from a later Persian king. Thus, what Daniel 9:1 shows us is that the throne-name Xerxes was in use well before the birth of Xerxes I of Persia and was applied to other kings before his reign. This being the case, it could well be that Cyrus, Cambyses II, and Darius were also called Xerxes on occasion and could be so called by the Jewish writers.

Summary and Conclusion

What all of this shows can be summarized as follows:

1. It is theoretically possible that the Persian monarchs used more than one name for themselves since these were all throne-names having descriptive meanings. All

The Names of the Persian Kings

extant evidence, however, shows the Persians calling these monarchs by one name each.

2. In interpreting the Bible, we have to be open to the fact that the Jews had their own names for the kings of other cultures and often used the same throne-name for more than one king. It is very likely that the Jewish theologians who wrote these texts used these throne-names with theological purposes in mind.

3. We have to take the Biblical references in their *Biblical* contexts, in this case the genealogical information and on that basis try to ascertain which monarch is in view.

Three
Genealogical Evidence in Ezra and Nehemiah

We now turn to the data that might help us positively identify the kings in Ezra-Nehemiah and Esther. These data must come from chronological considerations, which will indicate what time in history the events took place. The chronological information is contained in the genealogies, so to the often wearying task of discussing genealogies we must turn.

Many Bible readers do not realize that Ezra and Nehemiah are one book in the Hebrew Bible. At the end of each book in the Hebrew Masoretic text, the Hebrew scribes provide a count of the verses and a statement of the middle verse of the book. In the case of Ezra-Nehemiah, this information is lacking at the end of Ezra, and at the end of Nehemiah we are given a count of both books together, and the middle verse assumes a combined text.

Not only are Ezra and Nehemiah one book, but they almost certainly should be regarded as the last part of the book of Chronicles. The order of books in the Hebrew Bible is partly governed by liturgical considerations, and in the Hebrew Bible Chronicles comes after Ezra-Nehemiah. But as David Noel Freedman has written: "the present division into books (Chronicles-Ezra-Nehemiah) poses the question of the relationship of the former to the latter. The very fact that the books overlap (2 Chronicles 36:22-23 = Ezra 1:1-3a) would seem to settle the point: Ezra is the immediate sequel to Chronicles, and together they form part of the same original work.... It seems to me that the repetition of the verses is a late phenomenon, and the result of the division and ordering of the books in the Massoretic text, and has no immediate bearing on the question."[1]

As regards Ezra and Nehemiah, each book can stand alone. They are like twins. Ezra is concerned with holiness in the sanctuary, while Nehemiah is concerned with holiness in society. Ezra focuses on the Temple and its ethical boundaries; Nehemiah focuses on the city and its physical-symbolic boundary (the wall).

Both books have the same outline. In each we begin with a word from God's appointed sovereign, a word that authorizes the reestablishment of God's kingdom (Ezra 1-3; Neh. 1:1-2:16). In each book this is followed by a time of opposition, as enemies try to prevent the rebuilding of the Temple (Ezra) and wall (Nehemiah), but in each book God's people emerge victorious and the project is completed (Ezra 4:1-6:15; Neh. 2:17-6:19).

After the completion of the project, there is a formal covenant renewal, and associated with this are other events. In Ezra, the covenant renewal is followed by Ezra's visit to Jerusalem bringing spoils from the gentiles to adorn the Temple (Ezra 6:16-8:36). In Nehemiah, the covenant renewal is accompanied by a reorganization of the people and of their leaders (Neh. 7:1-13:3).

Virtually every time the covenant is renewed formally in the Old Testament, there is an immediate fall into sin. The first

---

1. *Divine Committment and Human Obligation*, Vol. 1 (Grand Rapids: Eerdmans, 1997), 89; from "The Chronicler's Purpose," orig. pub. *Catholic Biblical Quarterly* 23 (1961).

instance of this pattern is in Genesis 2–3, the next in Genesis 9, another in Genesis 15–16, again in Exodus 24 and 32, again in Leviticus 9–10, again in 2 Samuel 7 and 11, and again in both Ezra and Nehemiah. The "Fall and Renewal" in both books concerns the sin of intermarriage, the same sin committed by the Sethites before the Flood (Gen. 6; Ezra 9–10; Neh. 13:4–31).

Though these two books are twins, the fact that they are one book helps us to see that the rebuilding of the Temple is in fact not completed until the wall of the Holy City is built around it and that the rebuilding of the city actually begins when the exiles return and build the altar.

The Chronological Problem

The chronological problem in Ezra-Nehemiah boils down to this: On the one hand, the name lists in these two books lead us to expect that all the events in them took place in the reign of Darius; while on the other hand, the text calls the Persian emperor under whom Ezra and Nehemiah lived by the name "Artaxerxes," and Artaxerxes I (Artaxerxes Longimanus) reigned many years after Darius.

We can resolve this problem one of two ways. The first is to strain the information given in the name lists in order to make it fit, this approach being the common one. This gives us a long chronology for Ezra. The other way of resolving the problem is to hold that "Artaxerxes" in Ezra-Nehemiah is simply another name for Darius, giving us a short chronology.

In this chapter we examine the internal evidence in Ezra-Nehemiah, evidence that points to a short chronology.

Nehemiah and Mordecai

In Ezra 1–2, we read that immediately after Cyrus's decree (537 BC), a group of exiles returned from Babylon to begin work on the Lord's Temple. Among these were "Zerubbabel,

Jeshua, Nehemiah, Seraiah, Reelaiah, Mordecai," etc. (Ezra 2:2). Nehemiah 7:7 gives the same list: "Zerubbabel, Jeshua, Nehemiah, Azariah, Raamiah, Nahamani, Mordecai," etc. Who is this Nehemiah who returned with the first group of exiles? Most expositors hold that he cannot be the same as the Nehemiah who wrote Nehemiah, because the latter Nehemiah was still alive over one hundred years later.

We must ask, however, if this interpretation makes sense. What would the first audience of this text have understood? Of the names in Ezra 2:2 and Nehemiah 7:7, four directly correspond to important leaders of the post-exilic community: Zerubbabel, Jeshua, Nehemiah, Mordecai. Was the author trying to confuse his readers by mentioning some other Nehemiah and Mordecai in Ezra 2:2?

More, was Nehemiah trying to confuse us by mentioning some other Nehemiah in Nehemiah 7:7? Nehemiah himself introduces this list in 7:5. If some other Nehemiah were in view in the list, we are entitled to expect Nehemiah to have indicated that this is the case. We can compare Nehemiah 3:16, where we read about "Nehemiah the son of Azbuk, official of half the district of Beth-zur." This is clearly another Nehemiah, and that is why we are told who his father was. Nehemiah the governor carefully distinguishes this Nehemiah from himself. Surely he would have done the same in Nehemiah 7:7, if that Nehemiah had been someone other than himself.

We ought to assume that the Biblical writers were trying to communicate, not confuse. The reference to "Nehemiah" in Ezra 2:2 and Nehemiah 7:7 should be taken as strong evidence that the short chronology is correct. Nehemiah returned with the exiles and was present for the initial altar building under Joshua and Zerubbabel. At some later date he returned to Persia to serve King Darius-Artaxerxes.

Genealogical Evidence in Ezra and Nehemiah

We have noticed that Mordecai is also mentioned in Ezra 2:2 and Nehemiah 7:7. In the absence of any other qualifier, we should assume that this is *the* Mordecai, the great and renowned Mordecai of Esther 10:3. After all, how many Jewish leaders would have this Persian name? This identification would shorten the chronology as far as the book of Esther is concerned and indeed would tend to identify Esther's Ahasuerus as Darius.

Of course, it is possible some other Mordecai and Nehemiah are in view in these lists, but it is not likely. The only reason why so many expositors have made this assertion is because they were convinced that Artaxerxes Longimanus was the Persian monarch in the days of Ezra and Nehemiah.

Nehemiah 10 and 12

In Nehemiah 10 we are given a list of the priests and Levites who signed the covenant renewal document prepared by Nehemiah (Neh. 9:38). Most of the names on this list are identical with those who returned to Jerusalem at the time of Cyrus's decree. If the long chronology were correct, there would be a gap of about 91 years between these two events. According to the short chronology, there are only about 35 years between the two events.

Nehemiah 12:1–7 gives the names of the 22 chief priests who returned with Zerubbabel. Nehemiah 12:12–21 lists these same chief priests, omitting one, and sometimes the spelling is different. Nehemiah 10:1–8 lists 22 priests who signed the covenant in Nehemiah's 20th year. When we compare the list of 22 priests who signed the covenant with the 22 original chief priests, we find that 13, possibly 15, of the same names are found.

The list of covenant-signers in 10:1–8 does not follow the same order as the list of chief priests in 12:1–7 and 12–21, though they are roughly parallel. For one thing, the text does not say that the covenant-signers are chief priests, though since there are 22 of them, they probably each represent a particular priestly group. Second, it is likely that the list of covenant-signers simply records the names as they were recorded, and not in the order of the priestly courses.

In the following list, the column on the left is the list of 22 chief priests from 12:1–7, in order, with the alternate spellings from 12:12–21 in parenthesis. The column on the right lists the names that also occur in 10:1–8.

Priests

Nehemiah 12:1–7	Nehemiah 10:1–8
1. Seraiah	Seraiah
2. Jeremiah	Jeremiah
3. Ezra	(Azariah)
4. Amariah	Amariah
5. Malluch (Malluchi)	Malluch
6. Hattush	Hattush
7. Shechaniah (Shebaniah)	Shebaniah
8. Rehum (Harim)	Harim
9. Meremoth (Meraioth)	Meremoth
10. Iddo	—
11. Ginnetho (Ginnethon)	Ginnethon
12. Abijah	Abijah
13. Mijamin (Minjamin)	Mijamin
14. Maadiah (Moadiah)	(Maaziah)
15. Bilgah	Bilgai
16. Shemaiah	Shemaiah
17. Joiarib	—
18. Jedaiah	—
19. Sallu (Sallai)	—
20. Amok	—
21. Hilkiah	—

22. Jedaiah   —

A similar comparison can be made as regards the Levites:

Levites

Nehemiah 12:8–9	*Nehemiah 10:9*
1. Jeshua	Jeshua
2. Binnui	Binnui
3. Kadmiel	Kadmiel
4. Sherebiah	Shebaniah
5. Judah	(Hodijah, Ezra 2:40,3:9)
6. Mattaniah	—
7. Bakbukiah	—
8. Unni	—
(and 12 others)	

Of the eight Levites who are mentioned as returning with Zerubbabel, five are mentioned as signing the covenant with Nehemiah. Of the twenty-two priests who returned with Zerubbabel, thirteen, possibly fifteen, signed the covenant with Nehemiah. It is quite natural that twenty out of thirty men who returned with Zerubbabel in the first year of Cyrus should still be alive 34 years later. It is not reasonable to suppose that they would be alive 90 years later.

Expositors convinced of the long chronology get around this problem by saying that the names in Nehemiah 10 are family names, not personal names. That is, they are the names of the priestly courses established by the men living at the time of Zerubbabel, not the names of individuals. But this is precisely *not* said in Nehemiah 10:8. It only says of these men "these were the priests," in contrast to 12:7, which says "these were the heads of the priests." Moreover, a number of the names in Nehemiah 10:1–27 correspond to the personal names found in Nehemiah 3. Also, if family names or names of priestly courses are in view, then the two lists should be identical, which they are not. Of course, if it is a proven fact that the Artaxerxes of Nehemiah is Artaxerxes Longimanus, then some such explanation of Nehemiah 10 becomes necessary, but as we are seeking to show, there is good reason to suppose that the Artaxerxes in Nehemiah is in fact Darius. Therefore, Nehemiah 10 can stand without such an interpretation's being forced upon it.

Moreover, the post-exilic Jewish community was very concerned with genealogy, as 1 Chronicles 1–8 shows. The lists of names in Ezra-Nehemiah make the same point. Additionally, this concern is shown in Ezra 2:62, where we read, "These searched their ancestral registration, but they could not be located; therefore, they were considered unclean and out of the priesthood." If genealogy is so important, why would there be "gaps" and mere "family names" included? Clearly, the concern was to establish who was who, generation by generation. In this regard, consider the detailed information on the priests in Nehemiah 12:12–21.

The Priestly Genealogy

Jeshua the high priest, who returned with Zerubbabel, was not a young man at the time. We know this because his father, Jehozadak, was taken into captivity (1 Chron. 6:15). This was 50 years before the decree of Cyrus (2 Kings 25:18–22, by implication). Jehozadak's father Seraiah, slain by Nebuchadnezzar (2 Kings 25:18–22), was high priest at the time, so his father Azariah (1 Chron. 6:14) was already dead. Thus, Seraiah was probably in his 50s or 60s, which would put his eldest son Jehozadak in his 30s or 40s. Accordingly, it is likely that Jeshua was born before the captivity. It is possible that Jeshua was born in captivity, but he would still be fairly old by the 6th year of Darius, 21 years after the return, 71 years after the captivity. To be on the safe side, we shall put his age at 80 in the 6th year of Darius, 21 years after the return.

Jeshua's son was Joiakim (Neh. 12:10). He was high priest in the days of Ezra and Nehemiah (Neh. 12:26). It would appear that Jeshua died the year the Temple was completed. According to the long chronology, Nehemiah arrived in Jerusalem 71 years later than the 6th year of Darius, which would mean that Joiakim was born when his father was very old indeed, or else there is a gap in the genealogy. Gaps do appear in some genealogies in the Old Testament, but given the tremendous importance placed on the genealogical records of the priests and Levites in Ezra and Nehemiah, it is very unlikely that there is any gap here (Ezra 2:62; Neh. 12:22).

Of course, a gap is barely possible, but it is much easier to account for this genealogy on the basis of the short chronology. Old Jeshua died immediately after the Temple was dedicated, which means that his son Joiakim took over at the time Ezra arrived a year later.[2]

Joiakim's son was Eliashib (Neh. 12:10). Evidently, at the time of Nehemiah (13 years after Ezra arrived) Joiakim was already an old man, so his son Eliashib was helping him as high priest (Neh. 3:1). If Jeshua were 80 years old the year before Ezra arrived, Joiakim might have been 60 at that time and about 73 when Nehemiah arrived.

We are told of two sons of Eliashib: Joiada (Neh. 12:10), who served first as high priest, and Johanan (Neh. 12:23; Ezra 10:6), who served with and after him.

---

2. The death of the high priest is significant in establishing the nation; see Numbers 35:28, Numbers 20:22–21:3, and Joshua 24:33. The apparent fact that Jeshua's life spanned the entire captivity-punishment of Israel adds an additional dimension to Zechariah 3, where that punishment-defilement is removed from Jeshua as a sign that the period of defilement is over.

Darius, Artaxerxes, and Ahasuerus in the Bible

One of Joiada's sons, unnamed, was already married when Nehemiah returned for his last visit about 13 years later (Neh.13:28). We know that Joiada had a son named Jonathan, who is not listed in Nehemiah 12:22 as serving as high priest, though Jonathan's son Jaddua did serve (Neh. 12:11). Perhaps it was Jonathan who was cast out by Nehemiah, and perhaps that prevented his serving as high priest.[3]

It is helpful to realize that Johanan was Joiada's younger brother, because letters from the Jewish colony at Elephantine (see below) mention Johanan as a high priest in the fourteenth and seventeenth years of Darius's reign. If Johanan had been a son of Joiada, this would be impossible. According to Ezra 10:6, Johanan already had a room in the Temple precincts in the 7th year of Darius, so he must have been at least in his late teens at this time.

There is plenty of time for all this in the short chronology:

Darius year 6	Jeshua, age 80, dies;
	Joiakim, age 60;
	Eliashib, age 40;
	Joiada, age 20;
	Johanan, age 18
Darius year 7	Johanan, age 19, has room in Temple (Ezra 10:6)
Darius year 14	Johanan, age 26, has title of high priest, according to Elephantine letters. Johanan could have been apprenticing at this age. (Numbers 8:24, assuming that this rule for the Levites applied to the priests as well).

---

3. Some readers may be confused by these names. Though Johanan and Jonathan look similar in English, they are definitely not the same name in Hebrew. The English New Testament translates "Johanan" as "John."

Genealogical Evidence in Ezra and Nehemiah

Darius year 17	Johanan, age 29, has title of high priest, according to Elephantine letters.
Darius year 20	Nehemiah arrives;
	Joiakim, age 74;
	Eliashib, age 54;
	Joiada, age 34;
	Johanan, age 32;
	Joiada's unnamed son (Jonathan?), age 14.
Darius year 33	Nehemiah's second visit;
	Eliashib, age 67;
	Joiada, age 47;
	Johanan, age 45;
	Joiada's son (Jonathan?), married, age 27;
	Jaddua, age 2.

There was a Jewish colony in Egypt on an island in the Nile called in Greek Elephantine. Archaeologists have uncovered a number of legal documents and letters addressed to various persons in the Persian empire from this colony. A number of them are dated in the years of Darius, and these letters refer to people mentioned in Nehemiah: Bigvai (Neh. 7:19); Johanan the high priest; Hanani (Nehemiah's brother? Nehemiah 1:2); Sanballat (Neh. 3:1) (Papyri 21-22, 30-34). Because the present scholarly opinion is that Ezra and Nehemiah lived in the time of Artaxerxes Longimanus, it is assumed that the Darius of the Elephantine Papyri must be Darius II, who followed Longimanus. In terms of the short chronology, however, these letters should be understood as having been written in the time of Darius the Great.

It is interesting to notice that in Elephantine Papyrus No. 21 we have a letter to the head of the Elephantine colony, Yedoniah, from Hananiah, who might be Nehemiah's brother. The letter instructs them that King Darius had ordered in his 5th year that the Jews were to celebrate Passover. This squares very nicely with Ezra 5.

The Jaddua Question

Above I posited a date around 492 BC for the birth of Jaddua the High Priest. According to Josephus, *Antiquities of the Jews* 11:8, this same Jaddua was alive at the time Alexander the Great came to Jerusalem (c. 332 BC). If the thesis of this monograph is correct, Josephus is wrong. If Jaddua were born late in the reign of Artaxerxes Longimanus, say around 430 BC, it is possible that he was a very, very old man at the time of Alexander's visit to Jerusalem.

There are serious problems with Josephus's account of the Persian period, however. He seems to skip over most of the last 90 or so years of Persian history, omitting any events that took place during the reigns of the later kings until the end. It appears that Josephus assumed a shorter chronology for the Persian empire than is acceptable to modern scholars. We know when Alexander began his conquests, and we have a pretty thorough history of Greece stretching back from that date to the wars of Greece against Xerxes I, and before him, Darius. In other words, there is no good reason to doubt the conventional "BC" dates for the period of the Persian empire.

There is good reason to think, therefore, that Josephus is confused. The Bible chronologist Martin Anstey wrote: "It is very difficult to give an account of Josephus's view of the history of the Persian period. It is just the kind of history that would remain, if that of the Books of Ezra, Nehemiah, and Esther were 'emended,' 'corrected,' and interpolated by some later copyist or editor with a view to bringing it into accord with some other version of history. The result is a mixture of Scriptural events

Genealogical Evidence in Ezra and Nehemiah

attributed to the wrong persons as would follow from incorrect identifications of the persons named in the narrative."[4]

Recall that according to Josephus, the Artaxerxes of Ezra-Nehemiah was Xerxes I, who succeeded Darius (*Antiquities* 11:5:1). Since Xerxes I only reigned 21 years, right away we can see that Josephus is in error, since the Artaxerxes of Ezra-Nehemiah ruled for at least 32 years according to Nehemiah 13:6. But according to Josephus's confusions, Jaddua would have been born in the latter days of Nehemiah, let us say in the supposed 30th year of Xerxes I's reign, around 456 BC, which would make him about 120 years of age at the time of Alexander. Yet Josephus tells us that Jaddua's brother Manasseh had recently married a foreign woman at the time Alexander arrived, which means Jaddua was not all that old himself. Such confusions as these make Josephus a very unreliable source of information about these times.

Josephus's account of the meeting of Jaddua and Alexander is also problematic and with good reason is regarded as legend or fiction by scholars; to wit: when he encountered Jaddua, Alexander saluted him and then explained that he had seen Jaddua in a dream. Afterwards, Alexander went to the Temple and offered sacrifice to God. Then the prophecies in the book of Daniel about him were read to him, and he rejoiced to hear them.

Josephus may well have been right that the high priest at the time of Alexander was named Jaddua, but as scholars have pointed out, he may well have been a later Jaddua, since the names of the high priests recur throughout their genealogy.

---

4. Martin Anstey, *The Romance of Bible Chronology* (London: Marshall Brothers, 1913), 264. [Reprinted as *Chronology of the Old Testament* (Grand Rapids: Kregel, 1973).]

Josephus would merely have been wrong to associate this later Jaddua with the Jaddua of Nehemiah's day.

Thus, Josephus's statement that the Jaddua of the time of Alexander was the Jaddua of Nehemiah cannot be taken as serious evidence regarding the question before us.

The Ezra Question

As we saw above, the high priest at the time Nebuchadnezzar destroyed Jerusalem was Seraiah, and he was killed at that time. He was the father of Jeshua, who 71 years later presided over the Passover in the 6th year of Darius (Ezra 6). If we compare the genealogy of the high priests in 1 Chronicles 6:3-15 with the genealogy of Ezra in Ezra 7:1-5, we find that Ezra was a member of the high priestly family. His genealogy is identical with that of Seraiah, and he is said to be a son of Seraiah (Ezra 7:1). We have supposed that Jeshua was 80 in the 6th year of Darius. The youngest Ezra could possibly be at that time is 71, assuming he was born the year his father died.

Long chronologists argue that Ezra lived in the time of Artaxerxes Longimanus, not in the time of Darius the Great. Thus, they suppose a gap between Seraiah and Ezra in the genealogy of Ezra 7:1. They defend this supposition by pointing to the fact that there is a definite gap between Azariah and Meraioth in Ezra 7:3 (cp. 1 Chron. 6:7-10). If there is one gap in Ezra's genealogy, they point out, there may well be another.

Yet, this is a gap that is filled in by 1 Chronicles 6:7-10, and if Chronicles-Ezra-Nehemiah were one book originally, there was no need for the author to provide another complete genealogy in Ezra 7:1-5. Moreover, the genealogy of Ezra in Ezra 7:1-5 contains 17 names, including Ezra, going back to Aaron. The number 17 is symbolically significant in the Bible (7+10) and is used quite often. Books 3 and 4 of the Psalter, for instance, each contain 17 psalms. It seems, then, that the gap in Ezra's

Genealogical Evidence in Ezra and Nehemiah

genealogy is not an accident and should not be taken as license to suppose other gaps, especially since the author is so concerned with accurate genealogy for the priesthood.

Let us see whether the short chronology can successfully overcome the supposed gap between Seraiah and Ezra. Ezra was still alive in the 20th year of Darius, when Nehemiah arrived, making him at least 85 years old. Ezra was present at the dedication of the wall built under Nehemiah's supervision (Neh. 8:2). It only took 52 days for the wall to be rebuilt (Neh. 6:15), so that it was built in the very year Nehemiah arrived in Jerusalem. Thus, Ezra was 85 years old at this time. This is possible, and so no gap is needed. Ezra was the son of Seraiah, and brother of Jeshua the high priest.

Conclusion

We have examined genealogical evidence that favors a short chronology for Ezra-Nehemiah, so that the Artaxerxes of Ezra 7–10 and Nehemiah is Darius. The genealogical evidence is much easier to account for on the assumption of a short chronology, and there is no evidence that necessitates a long chronology.

Four
The Persian Kings in Ezra 4–6

Ezra 4:6–23 recounts that the enemies of the Jews wrote letters and opposed the rebuilding of the Temple during the reigns of Ahasuerus and Artaxerxes. This information is inserted between the statement that "they hired counsellors against them to frustrate their counsel all the days of Cyrus king of Persia, even until the reign of Darius king of Persia" (4:5); and the statement, "and work on the house of God in Jerusalem ceased, and it was stopped until the second year of Darius king of Persia" (4:24).

A "common sense" reading of Ezra 4 would lead us to suppose that after Cyrus came a king called Ahasuerus and then another called Artaxerxes and then Darius. During the reigns of Ahasuerus and Artaxerxes, work on the Temple was forbidden. It used to be assumed that Ahasuerus was Cambyses II, and Artaxerxes was Pseudo-Smerdis.

Modern exegetes assume that the information about Ahasuerus and Artaxerxes is dischronologized. They assume that the kings are Xerxes I and Artaxerxes Longimanus and that the letters of opposition sent during the reigns of these later kings have been put into the text of Ezra at this point for thematic reasons. They assume this is the case because they believe that the Artaxerxes of Ezra-Nehemiah is Artaxerxes Longimanus. If the Artaxerxes of Ezra-Nehemiah is Darius, however, this modern assumption cannot stand. The purpose of the present chapter is to take up this problem.

Artaxerxes in Ezra 6:14

We shall begin by looking first at Ezra 6:14. Here we read that the Jews finished building "according to the command of the God of Israel and the decree of Cyrus and Darius and Artaxerxes king of Persia." The problem with this verse is that the only decree of "Artaxerxes" mentioned in Ezra to this point is in 4:7–23, which was a decree to stop building the city! Moreover, if the Artaxerxes of Ezra 6:14 is Longimanus, it is curious that he is mentioned here because the rest of Ezra says nothing about any decree of his to rebuild the temple. Of course, if Nehemiah is considered part of Ezra, then we can say that this is a decree to rebuild the wall of Jerusalem, but then the question is: why is this mentioned here in Ezra 6:14?

The modern answer is, again, for thematic reasons: Artaxerxes (Longimanus) is mentioned here, even though he had nothing to do with rebuilding the Temple in the days of Haggai, Zechariah, Zerubbabel, and Jeshua, simply because later on he will order the walls of the city to be rebuilt. To say the least, this is a very odd and confusing way for the author of Ezra to write.

A far simpler solution is found in Hebrew grammar itself, which allows for "and" to mean "even" or "to wit." In that case, Ezra 6:14 would read, "according to . . . the decree of Cyrus and Darius, to wit: Artaxerxes." Here is Gesenius's explanation of this use of the connective "and" in Hebrew: "Frequently *vav copulativum* [the connective 'and'] is also *explanatory* (like *isque*, *et-quidem*, and the German *und zwar*, the English *to wit*), and is then called *vav explicativum* [the explicative 'and']. For instance, Isaiah 17:8 reads, 'Nor will he look to that which his fingers have made, to wit: the Asherim and incense stands.' Similarly, Nehemiah 8:13 reads, 'the [people] gathered around Ezra the scribe, to wit: to give attention to the words of the Law.' In Proverbs 3:12: 'For whom the Lord loves He reproves, even [to wit] as a father the son in whom he delights.' "[1]

This reading of Ezra 6:14 is not new. John Gill, in his commentary (late 18th century) writes, "I am most inclined to think, with Aben Ezra [noted Jewish commentator], that he [Artaxerxes] is Darius himself; and the words to be read, Darius, that is, Artaxerxes, king of Persia; Artaxerxes being, as he [Aben Ezra] observes, a common name [throne-name] of the kings of Persia, as Pharaoh was of the kings of Egypt . . . and I find Dr. Lightfoot [an eminent Puritan chronologist] was of the same mind."

The use of an explicative "and" is clear in 1 Chronicles 5:26, "The God of Israel stirred up the spirit of Pul king of Assyria, and [that is:] the spirit of Tiglath-pileser king of Assyria." Scholars beginning with D. J. Wiseman have argued that Daniel 6:28 should be read the same way: "Daniel prospered in the reign of Darius and [that is:] in the reign of Cyrus the Persian."[2] As Colless points out, the Hebrew writer had available a clearer way of writing this sentence if he wanted to distinguish Darius and Cyrus, as seen in Ezra 4:5-6, "all the days of Cyrus king of Persia

---

1. See *Gesenius's Hebrew Grammar*, second English ed. (Oxford U. Press), 484n1b.
2. See Brian Colless, "Cyrus the Persian as Darius the Mede in the Book of Daniel," *Journal for the Study of the Old Testament* 56 (1992), 113-26; D. J. Wiseman, *Notes on Some Problems in the Book of Daniel* (London: Tyndale Press, 1965).

Darius, Artaxerxes, and Ahasuerus in the Bible

and *until/into* the reign of Darius king of Persia."[3] In both of these cases, the explicative use of *waw* is used to identify two names as belonging to the same foreign king, establishing that this way of writing was known and employed by Jewish writers.

Remembering that the Bible often uses names meaningfully, we can interpret Ezra and Nehemiah in terms of the meaning of the names Darius and Artaxerxes. Ezra 6 would use the name Darius to focus on the fact that the king was doing good: "Then King Do-good issued a decree" (Ezra 6:1). Ezra 7 would shift to the name Artaxerxes to focus on the justice and universality of the king's reign. Notice the end of Darius's letter in 6:12, "I Darius (the Doer) issue decree; let it be *done* diligently." Now compare the end of Artaxerxes' letter in Ezra 7:25–26, "Set magistrates and judges who may judge . . . all such as know the laws of your God. . . . Whoever will not observe the law of your God and the law of the king, let judgment be executed speedily on him." The emphasis on justice is in keeping with the meaning of the name Artaxerxes (King of Justice).

Since the genealogical and name-list evidence strongly indicate a short chronology for Ezra and Nehemiah, there is every reason to assume that Darius and Artaxerxes are the same person.

Ahasuerus in Ezra 4:6

We have seen that it is likely that the Artaxerxes of Ezra-Nehemiah is the same as Darius the Great. If this solution be correct, and I think it is, possibly there is another problem in Ezra that can be resolved by it. In Ezra 4:6 we are told that "in the reign of Ahasuerus, at the beginning of his reign, they wrote an accusation against the inhabitants of Judah and Jerusalem." Nothing more is ever said about this accusation. The next verse

---

3. Ibid., 115n3.

reads, "And in the days of Artaxerxes" they wrote a letter of accusation. A full discussion of this letter ensues in Ezra 4. There are several interpretations of these verses.

A. The common interpretation says that Ahasuerus is Xerxes I and Artaxerxes is Longimanus. It is held that the letters to these two later monarchs are mentioned here, out of chronological sequence, because the theme of this section of Ezra is in opposition to God's work. Thus, we are shown two later instances of opposition.

B. The classical interpretation is that Ahasuerus is Cambyses II and Artaxerxes is Pseudo-Smerdis. We know that there are at least two Ahasueruses in the Bible (Dan. 9:1; Esth. 1:1), so why not a third? The value of the classical interpretation is that it does not wrench Ezra 4 out of chronological sequence, nor does it fall into the modern trap of assuming that the Jews called these monarchs by only one name each and that they used the same names the Greeks used. The problem with the classical interpretation is that Pseudo-Smerdis almost certainly did not reign long enough for a letter to have reached him and a reply to have been sent back.

C. Another view is that Ahasuerus is Cambyses II and Artaxerxes is Darius. This makes a lot of sense, since as we have seen it is likely that in Ezra-Nehemiah, Darius and Artaxerxes are the same king. The scenario presented is that at the beginning of Cambyses II's reign, a letter of complaint was sent to him, which he ignored. Then again, at the beginning of Darius's reign, when he was threatened with insurrection on all sides, more letters were sent complaining about the Jews. Darius-Artaxerxes ordered work on the Temple stopped. In the 2nd year of his reign, having received more information, Darius ordered the work resumed (Ezra 6).

D. Another twist on this is to see both Ahasuerus and Artaxerxes as Cambyses II, so that Ezra 4:7ff. is simply filling out 4:6. This means, however, that within Ezra's book there are two Artaxerxeses (4:6 and 6:14) and that they are not distinguished by any indication—an unlikely thing for a writer to do.

E. Finally there is my view. I suggest that the Ahasuerus of Ezra 4:6 and the Artaxerxes of 4:7 are both Darius, and that the "and" of 4:7 should be translated "to wit." This means that the phrase "at the beginning of his reign" applies to Darius-Artaxerxes and that the letter sent to Artaxerxes in Ezra 4:7 is the same as the one sent to Ahasuerus in 4:6. It also means that Ezra 4:5-6 are in chronological order. To wit: "They hired counselors against them to frustrate their counsel all the days of Cyrus king of Persia, even until the reign of Darius (Do-good) king of Persia. To wit, in the reign of Ahasuerus (Chief of Rulers, Darius–Artaxerxes), in the beginning of his reign, they wrote an accusation against the inhabitants of Judah and Jerusalem. To wit, in the days of Artaxerxes (Kingdom of Justice, Darius), Bishlam, Mithredath, Tabeel, and the rest of his colleagues, wrote to Artaxerxes king of Persia; and the text of the letter was written in Aramaic and translated from Aramaic."

My conclusion is that either Ahasuerus is Cambyses II and Artaxerxes is Darius, or that both are Darius. For reasons to be explored in chapter 5 of this monograph, I am convinced that the Ahasuerus of Esther is Darius. He certainly cannot be Cambyses II. For that reason, I think it most likely that the author of Ezra is simply linking these three names together as names for the same person: Darius the Great.

The Letter of Ezra 4

The letter in Ezra 4 complains that the Jews were rebuilding not the Temple but the wall. The long chronology says that under Darius the Temple was rebuilt, but that when the Jews began to rebuild the wall, stiff opposition arose against them. In the days of Xerxes I (son of Darius) and in the days of Artaxerxes Longimanus they were prevented from rebuilding the wall.

The Persian Kings in Ezra 4–6

Finally, Nehemiah obtained permission to rebuild the wall, in the 20th year of Artaxerxes Longimanus.

I believe that there is internal Biblical evidence against this reconstruction. We have seen that it is most likely that the Artaxerxes of Ezra-Nehemiah is Darius. But if the wall was not rebuilt until Nehemiah came in Darius's 20th year, why were letters sent complaining about the wall at the beginning of Darius's reign? The answer is seen in Ezra 9:9, which says that the Jews had begun rebuilding the wall before Nehemiah and indeed had erected some kind of a wall by the time Ezra arrived in Jerusalem.

Here is the historical scenario, as I see it: Jews returned to Jerusalem in the first year of Cyrus. They built the altar, and begin rebuilding the temple (Ezra 3). Soon, however, they encountered opposition, which "discouraged them and frightened them from building" (Ezra 4:4). The people left off working on the temple and devoted themselves to building nice homes for themselves and working on the wall (Haggai 1). God eventually raised up adversaries who complained about this wall-building, and at the beginning of his reign Darius forbade them to work on the wall and city (Ezra 4:21). They were not, however, forbidden to work on the temple. Haggai told them that they were in sin for not having finished the temple first (Haggai 1). No longer able to work on walls and houses, the people devoted themselves to rebuilding the temple. This aroused more questions, and another letter was sent to Darius asking about the temple (Ezra 5). Darius gave permission to rebuild the temple, which was completed in the 6th year of Darius (Ezra 6). The next year Ezra arrived and noted that both the temple and a rudimentary wall had been completed.

This scenario does better justice to the information contained in the texts of Ezra-Nehemiah and Haggai and does not require that Ezra 4 be yanked out of historical context.

Five
The Setting of the Book of Esther

We now turn to a consideration of the king in Esther, who is called Ahasuerus. Paton writes, "On this point until recently [1908] opinions have differed widely. Every king of Media and Persia, from Cyaxeres to Artaxerxes Ochus, has been selected by some one for identification with this monarch."[1] Paton proceeds to summarize all the various proposed identifications. In this chapter, we shall only look at those that have been advocated in recent years. The most popular view is that he is Xerxes I. I shall argue that he is Darius.

Xerxes I

The reason Xerxes I is favored is that "Ahasuerus" is the Hebrew equivalent of the Greek "Xerxes," both versions of the Persian "Khshyarsha." This link has led modern commentators to assume that they must be the same man. By itself, this is not enough, though, because as we have seen Daniel 9:1 says that "Darius the Mede" was the son of Ahasuerus. Thus, as far as the

---

1. Lewis Bayles Paton, *A Critical and Exegetical Commentary on the Book of Esther,* International Critical Commentary (Edinburgh: T. & T. Clark, 1980), 51.

Darius, Artaxerxes, and Ahasuerus in the Bible

Jewish writers were concerned, there was more than one Ahasuerus.

Other arguments favoring Xerxes I are these:

1. The period during which Xerxes I was occupied with his Grecian campaign seems to correspond to the four-year gap in the book of Esther (1:3; 2:16).
2. The banquet held in Ahasuerus' third year seems to correspond to that held at Xerxes I's great council (Herodotus 7:8).
3. The palatial details attested to in Esther seem identical to those archaeologically uncovered at Susa, Xerxes I's capital.

These arguments, and other lesser ones, are, however, far from decisive:

1. Darius also was involved in campaigns in the early years of his reign.
2. There were rebellions at the beginning of Darius's reign which took him a couple of years to put down, after which we can expect that he held a festival.
3. Susa was a capital city of Persia under Cyrus and Cambyses II, but particularly under Darius, who built his palace there, which was already occupied in 521 BC. This palace was certainly ready for a festival by 519 BC. A. T. Olmstead's *History of the Persian Empire*[2] reproduces Darius's own description of the palace, mentioning cedar and teak, gold, lapis lazuli, carnelian, turquoise, silver, copper, ivory, as well as the inlay

---

2. Chicago: U. of Chicago, 1948, 168.

work. Everything indicates the same kind of opulence described in Esther 1.

Evidence in the Bible, however, makes the Xerxes I identification difficult if not impossible. To begin with, as we have seen, Ezra 2:2 lists Mordecai as one of the grown men who returned to Jerusalem right after the decree of Cyrus. It is hardly likely that many Jewish men were named "Man of Marduk," a pagan god; and it is also unlikely that the book of Ezra would mention some other Mordecai without explaining who he was.

We have argued that the Artaxerxes of Ezra-Nehemiah is Darius. We have argued that the Ahasuerus of Ezra-Nehemiah is the same man, thus possibly identifying Esther's king as Darius-Artaxerxes. We noted in chapter 1 of this study that both Josephus and the Greek version of Esther call the king Artaxerxes. Josephus assumes that he was Artaxerxes Longimanus. Josephus probably drew this assumption from the Greek version of Esther. The authors of the Greek version, however, do not link their Artaxerxes with Longimanus. Rather, the translators assume that Artaxerxes is properly a good translation of Ahasuerus, a legitimate alternate name for this king, whoever he was.

We must now take note of the genealogical notice in Esther 2:5-6, "There was a Jew in Susa the capital whose name was Mordecai, the son of Jair, the son of Shimei, the son of Kish, a Benjaminite; who had been taken into exile from Jerusalem with the captives who had been exiled with Jeconiah (Jehoiachin) king of Judah, whom Nebuchadnezzar the king of Babylon had exiled."

There are two possible ways to read this text. One is that Mordecai, whose genealogy is sketched, was taken into captivity. The other is that Kish, great-grandfather of Mordecai, was taken into captivity. C. F. Keil argues that it must be Mordecai who was taken into captivity: "It is more in accordance with the

Hebrew narrative style to refer [the word *who*] to the chief person of the sentence preceding it, viz., Mordochai, who also continues to be spoken of in v. 7."[3] Paton is more blunt writing that Hebrew usage "demands the reference of *who* to Mordecai. The appositives *ben Jair, ben Shimei, ben Kish*, like Johnson or Jackson, serve merely as surnames for Mordecai."[4]

Moreover, few commentators doubt that the Kish and Shimei referred to are not grandfather and great-grandfather of Mordecai, but are the father of Saul and the enemy of David, distant ancestors of Mordecai. They are mentioned to show that Esther is of royal Benjaminite blood and that the conflict between Saul and Agag (1 Samuel 15; Haman the Agagite) is rejoined in Esther.

Thus, this statement says that Mordecai was taken into captivity with Jehoiachin in the 8th year of Nebuchadnezzar's reign (2 Kings 24:12; 597 BC). If Mordecai was an infant at this time, he would be about 61 when Cyrus issued his decree and when Mordecai made his initial return to Jerusalem (Ezra 2:2; 537 BC). At the beginning of Darius's reign (522 BC), Mordecai would be 77, and he would be 89 in Darius's 12th year, which is when Esther ends. But if we want to pull all this down to the reign of Xerxes I, Mordecai would have to be about 113 at the beginning of that emperor's reign and 125 in his 12th year!

Accordingly, Keil and modern expositors assume that it was not Mordecai himself who was taken into captivity as a child or infant, but that he came into captivity "in the loins" of his parents or grandparents. This, however, is a forced interpretation that does not arise from the text, but is grasped from theology, and made necessary by the assumption that Xerxes I is the king in Esther. As

---

3. In Keil & Delitzsch, *Old Testament Commentary, ad loc.*
4. Paton, 168.

The Persian Kings in Ezra 4–6

Paton writes, "the fact remains that *who was carried captive* is not a natural way of saying *whose ancestors were carried captive*."[5]

Paton's conclusion: "Most recent commentators frankly admit that the author has here made a blunder in his chronology."[6] Our conclusion, of course, is that Ahasuerus is not Xerxes I but Darius.

Esther was Mordecai's niece, but Esther 2:7 indicates that she was much younger then he, so that she was like a daughter to him. In large families, it is not unusual for a man to be older than his uncle. Assuming that this is the scenario, Esther might be 40 years younger than Mordecai. This would make her 43 when she became queen. If she was 55 years younger than Mordecai, she would have been 28 when she became queen, assuming Ahasuerus is Darius. This is possible.

For this scenario to work, we can assume that Mordecai was the first son of his grandfather's firstborn, while Esther's father was the last son of Mordecai's grandfather. Thus, while Mordecai's father and Esther's father were brothers, they were perhaps 25 years apart in age, and Mordecai was perhaps 5 years older than his uncle. (I myself am 50 at the time I write this, and I have a cousin who is in his 90s. His children are 10 to 15 years older than I am. I had uncles and aunts who were more than 60 years older than I.)

Now, Esther's father and mother are both dead. If we assume that they did not die violently, we can assume that Esther was one of their later children, born perhaps when her father was 50. This would make Esther 55 years younger than Mordecai, her cousin.

This scenario is not strained at all, and squares with the tightest reading of the Hebrew text; to wit: that Mordecai was

---

5. Ibid., 169.
6. Idem.

brought into captivity with Jehoiachin and that Mordecai was a leader of the Jewish community at the time of the return from Exile (Ezra 2:2).

We have sought to establish the following:

1. The book of Ezra-Nehemiah does not skip from Darius to Artaxerxes Longimanus, but uses "Artaxerxes" as a name for Darius.
2. The Mordecai mentioned in Ezra-Nehemiah must be the same as the Mordecai in Esther. It makes no sense to doubt this.
3. Mordecai was alive at the time of the captivity and could not have lived until the reign of Xerxes I.
4. The name "Xerxes" or Ahasuerus was held by more than one ruler and is likely given to Darius in Ezra 4:6.
5. Nothing in the scenario of Esther contradicts identifying Ahasuerus as Darius the Great.

We must now consider two other alternative suggestions.

Cambyses II

Herbert A. Storck has revived the suggestion that Ahasuerus might be Cambyses II, who ruled after Cyrus.[7] He argues that for Esther to be as much younger than Mordecai as is required for the Darius interpretation puts a strain on the text, so moving the time back to Cambyses II should be considered. He also argues that since Cambyses II ruled as co-regent with Cyrus, his reign can be considered to have lasted 15 rather than 7 or so years. Finally, filling out the scenario, he argues that Mordecai might have been a prominent Jewish merchant, and that there was a

---

7. *History and Cosmology: Studies in the Book of Esther* (Toronto: House of Nabu, 1990). See Paton, 52, for some earlier advocates of this view.

The Persian Kings in Ezra 4–6

rich banker in Babylon who had the name Itti Marduk balatu, who might have been Mordecai.

There are more problems with Storck's suggestion than there are with the Darius view however (and Storck only offers his view as a suggestion). First, Cambyses II clearly did not reign over 127 provinces (Esth. 1:1), and this information is given in Esther to help us identify which Ahasuerus is being referred to. Storck can only offer that "it could also refer to Cambyses II's reign, retrospectively." More than that, however, it is a fact that Darius conquered India; Cambyses II never ruled it. And Darius conquered the islands of the sea and levied tribute on them, something Cambyses II did not do. Thus, if Storck is correct, Cambyses II is being described as Darius!

Second, if Cambyses II was co-regent, it is hard to see how he could have put on such a huge feast in Susa in the third year of his and his father's reign. The feast of Esther 1 does not read like a festival put on by the mere son of a king.

Third, there is good evidence to believe that Cambyses II was opposed to the Jews. The 79 verses of Daniel 10–12 are all one long vision and revelation. The setting is the 3rd year of Cyrus. Daniel tells us that he had been mourning for 3 blocks of weeks, thus 3 full weeks, or 21 days. This period ended on the 20th day of the 1st month and thus crossed the entire Passover and Feast of Unleavened Bread season. During this time, Daniel ate no meat and drank no wine, thus not participating in any shadow observance of the feast in any way whatsoever. He did not eat "bread of desirability," which may mean choice bread, or might refer to unleavened bread. Finally, he used no ointment, which means he kept his body free from oils. Oil is used for anointing priests and kings in the Bible. By doing all of this, Daniel stressed that he was in exile from the bread and wine of God's kingdom, the anointing of God's work, the feasts of God's calendar.

Since Cyrus had decreed that the Temple be restored in his 1st year, clearly something had gone awry. The Temple had not been restored, as we know from Ezra 1–5.

Moreover, Daniel sees a "man dressed in linen, whose waist was girded with pure gold of Uphaz, whose body was like turquoise, whose face was like lightning, whose eyes were like flaming torches, whose arms and feet were like the gleam of polished bronze, and the sound of whose voice was like the sound of tumult." This "Man" was in the air above the river Tigris, at Babylon (12:7). Clearly this is Yahweh, and He is above the river just as He was above the River Chebar in Ezekiel 1. The meaning in Ezekiel was that God had departed from the Temple and had come to be with His people in exile. The meaning in Daniel 10–12 is that God is still in exile and has not returned to the Temple. He is, however, above the waters, like the Spirit in Genesis 1, and is preparing a new creation.

The problem is described in Ezra 4; to wit, that after the first year of return from exile, opposition to the Temple's rebuilding arose among the people then living in the area, and they hired representatives to go to the Persian court and put a stop to the project. As we have seen, they were successful throughout the reigns of Cyrus and Cambyses II and initially successful with Darius as well.

Since Cyrus was favorable to the Jews, it must have been Cambyses II who was not. Cyrus was off conquering new lands, and Cambyses II, the Prince of Persia, was basically in charge. In Daniel 11:1, the person who is speaking with Daniel says that "in the first year of Darius the Mede [Cyrus] I stood up to strengthen and protect him." Almost certainly this speaker is an angelic messenger. He says that there was some problem in the beginning of Cyrus's reign, but that he had stood up to help Cyrus. We now know from ancient records that Cambyses II was co-regent with Cyrus in Babylon initially, but was removed

The Persian Kings in Ezra 4–6

during Cyrus's first year. Since it seems clear that Cambyses II opposed the Temple-rebuilding project, the "strengthening" of Cyrus would seem to be connected with the removal of Cambyses II's opposition. Thereafter, in Cyrus's 1st year, the decree to rebuild the Temple was issued.[8]

Shea has argued cogently that Cambyses II became co-regent with Cyrus at the New Year Festival in the Spring of 535 BC, on the 4th day of the month. This was when Daniel went into mourning, in the 3rd year of Cyrus (Dan. 10:1–3).

In Daniel 10:13 and 20, the angel tells Daniel that he had been fighting the Prince of Persia for the 21 days of Daniel's mourning, but Michael, the Prince of Israel, had stood up to help him. Thus, he was able to gain a small victory. Soon he would be returning to oppose the Prince of Persia further. Often this Prince is said to be the angelic overlord of Persia, but Calvin identified him as the real prince, Cambyses II. Shea has demonstrated that Calvin was almost certainly correct.

In fact, the real overlord of Persia is the godly angel who has been opposing Cambyses II, and who has received help from the angelic overlord of Israel, the arch-angel (chief of angels) Michael, the pre-incarnate Christ. (That Michael is Christ follows from a comparison of Jude 9 with Zechariah 3:2.)

We don't really know all that we would like to know about the reign of the Persian kings, but from what I have just presented, it seems that Cambyses II is a long shot as far as being the Ahasuerus of Esther is concerned. If Mordecai is indeed to be linked to a prominent Jewish banking concern, we can be sure that this concern would still be in operation in Darius's day.

---

8. See William H. Shea, "Darius the Mede in His Persian-Babylonian Setting," *Andrews University Seminary Studies* 29 (1991), 235–57.

Astyages

E. W. Faulstich has sought to renew the universally-discarded notion that Ahasuerus was the Median king Astyages.[9] He presents his arguments in his book *History, Harmony, The Exile & Return*.[10] To understand it, we have to have some background.

The Assyrians ruled the near east. Median king Cyaxeres decided to make war on Assyria and enlisted the support of the governor of Babylon, which was under Assyrian rule. They succeeded in defeating Assyria, and Babylonia became a separate empire under her former governor, Nabopolassar, allied with Media. At this time, Persia was just a small kingdom.

Cyaxeres and Nabopolassar cemented their alliance with a marriage. The daughter of Cyaxeres, Amytis, married the son of Nabopolassar, Nebuchadnezzar, who built the famous hanging gardens of Babylon because Amytis missed the beautiful mountain scenery of Media.

Cyaxeres' son was Astyages, and he succeeded his father. Thus, Astyages ruled Media at the time when his brother-in-law Nebuchadnezzar ruled Babylon. Astyages also formed an alliance with the small kingdom of Persia, marrying his daughter Mandane to the Persian king Cambyses I. Their son was Cyrus the Great.

Now, Faulstich notes that according to Daniel 5, Belshazzar is regarded as the son of Nebuchadnezzar. He supposes that Belshazzar came to the throne when Nebuchadnezzar went insane for 7 "times," which he interprets as 7 years (Dan. 4). After 3 years of incompetent rule, Belshazzar was overthrown. At that time, Nebuchadnezzar's wife Amytis asked her brother Astyages to take over Babylon. Thus, Astyages ruled Babylon for the next 4 years, until Nebuchadnezzar was restored. According

---

9. For earlier advocates of either Cyraxeres or Astyages, see Paton, 52.
10. (Spencer, IA: Chronology Books, 1988).

to Faulstich, Astyages was "Darius the Mede" of the later parts of Daniel.

Now, this Darius was "son of Ahasuerus, of Median descent" according to Daniel 9:1. This would mean that the Median king Cyaxeres was this Ahasuerus. Faulstich assumes that "Ahasuerus" was a Median throne-name and thus was used by Astyages (his "Darius the Mede") as well.

Faulstich posits Astyages as the Ahasuerus of Esther. He substantiates this claim by insisting that Esther must have come into exile with her uncle Mordecai and thus would be far too old to have married any later Persian king.

What are we to make of this? In fact, Faulstich's proposal is a house of cards. First of all, there is nothing that even hints that Esther came into captivity with Mordecai. It is quite possible that Mordecai adopted Esther when he returned to Jerusalem in Ezra 2, in the second year of Cyrus. If she was a young orphan, he would have taken her in and then taken her back to Babylon and Susa with him. It is even possible that Mordecai was the person who transported the Jewish appeals mentioned in Ezra 4. At any rate, Faulstich has no grounds for his insistence that Esther was alive at the time of the initial exile.

Second, there is little doubt now that "Darius the Mede" is Cyrus himself, great-grandson of King Cyaxeres of Media. The Hebrew "Ahasuerus" is likely synonymous with the Greek "Cyaxeres," both corruptions of the Persian/Median "Uwaxshtra."

Third, the "queen" in Daniel 5 speaks to Belshazzar with authority and speaks of Nebuchadnezzar as his "father." Thus, it has reasonably been suggested that the queen is Belshazzar's mother, the wife of Nabonidus, and that she was a daughter of Nebuchadnezzar. (She is not Belshazzar's wife; Daniel 5:2.) Thus, even though Nabonidus was a "usurper," Belshazzar would be a grandson of Nebuchadnezzar. Thus, Faulstich's insistence that there were two Belshazzars, one the son of Nebuchadnezzar and the other the son of Nabonidus, cannot be sustained.

Fourth, it is sheer supposition that this "first Belshazzar" and then Astyages stood in for Nebuchadnezzar during his 7 years of insanity.

Fifth, while Daniel speaks of the "laws of the Medes and Persians," indicating that Media was still the dominant partner, Esther speaks of the "laws of the Persians and Medes" (Esth. 1:19). Moreover, Esther uses the phrase "Persia and Media" in 1:3, 14, and 18. This indicates that the events happened later on, after Persia became the dominant partner (which happened shortly into the reign of Cyrus). This phrase cannot possibly apply during the days of Astyages.

Sixth, Esther's king was able to order the extermination of the Jews throughout all 127 provinces of "his" empire, which according to Faulstich is the Babylonian Empire (!). This happened in the 12th year of his reign. By that time, according to Faulstich's view, Nebuchadnezzar was again of sound mind and ruling the Babylonian empire. How could the Median king issue such a command? Esther 8:9 and 9:30 say that the king ruled all 127 provinces at the time. How could this be, if Nebuchadnezzar was in charge?[11]

Seventh, if Nebuchadnezzar was in charge, how could Astyages levy a tax on the islands in Nebuchadnezzar's empire, as Esther 10 says?

---

11. According to Faulstich, Nebuchadnezzar was insane for 7 years. During the first 3, Belshazzar reigned in his stead. During the last 4, Astyages-Ahasuerus reigned in his stead. According to Esther 2:16, this king married Esther in his 7th year of reign, which we can count from the time he became king of Media. The attack on the Jews took place in his 12th year, which is 5 years later. This is one year after Nebuchadnezzar's recovery, so Astyages-Ahasuerus could not have been reigning Babylon at this time. Thus, even if we try to shorten the time Astyages ruled Babylon, we don't have enough time for Faulstich's proposal.

The Persian Kings in Ezra 4–6

Finally, Daniel 4 only says that Nebuchadnezzar was insane for 7 "times." These might have been months, not years. Thus, even a "seven-year insanity" for the Babylonian king is not clearly taught in the Bible.

Thus, Faulstich's reconstruction of events is impossible. Esther's king was Persian and was in charge of an empire that reached from Ethiopia to India. He could not have been an earlier Median ruler, nor could he have been standing in for Nebuchadnezzar for 12 years or even for 5 after Belshazzar's supposed 3 years.

Darius the Great

It seems that the only plausible choice for Esther's king is Darius the Great. History substantiates this in detail.

First, Darius had to spend the first two years of his reign putting down rebellions. Thus, a feast in his 3rd year is very likely.

Second, Darius then went on several campaigns, so returning to Susa and selecting a new wife in his 7th year is likely.

Third, Darius invaded and conquered India in 506 BC (Herodotus, Books 3 and 4). Darius inherited the conquests of his predecessor Cambyses II in Egypt and Ethiopia. He subdued the Ethiopians when they rebelled (Herodotus, Book 3).

Fourth, Darius's fleet took the islands of Samos, Chios, and Lesbos, and the rest of the islands in 496 BC (Herodotus, Book 6). In 3:89–97, Herodotus states that these islands paid tribute to Darius. Herodotus adds, "Later on in his reign the sum was increased by the tribute from the Islands and of the nations of Europe as far as Thessaly" (3:96). Thucydides (Book 1) and Plato (Menexenus) say that Darius subdued all the islands in the Aegean Sea, and Diodorus Siculus (Book 12) says that these were all lost again by his son Xerxes I before the 12th year of his reign, which eliminates the possibility that Xerxes I is the Ahasuerus of Esther.

Darius, Artaxerxes, and Ahasuerus in the Bible

Fifth, Darius was the Persian king who instituted economic reform, standardizing weights, measures, and coinage, and levying tribute upon the subject peoples.[12] The notice about levying tribute in Esther 10 cannot apply to any earlier king, and since it speaks of the institution of this levy, most likely refers to Darius.

Sixth, we have seen that Darius is called Artaxerxes in Ezra-Nehemiah. In the apocryphal additions to Esther, and in the Greek Septuagint translation throughout, Esther's king is called Artaxerxes.

Finally, in the apocryphal book 1 Esdras 3:1-2, we read, "Now King Darius gave a great banquet for all that were under him and all that were born in his house and all the nobles of Media and Persia and all the satraps and generals and governors that were under him in the 127 satrapies from India to Ethiopia." While the rest of this story is probably fiction, the description of the banquet seems to come directly from Esther, and we note that the king is Darius.

Thus, for all of these reasons, and especially since no one else is a possibility, it is clear that the Ahasuerus of Esther is Darius the Great.

In Nehemiah 2:6, we read that Nehemiah, cupbearer to King Darius-Artaxerxes, made his request, and the queen was sitting beside the king. Nothing more is said about this queen. There is no queen who would be of interest to the first readers of Nehemiah except Esther, and there is no other queen of interest to us either.[13]

---

12. Olmstead, 185ff.

13. It should be noted, though, that Nehemiah does not mention the queen simply to titillate our curiosity about who she might be. In Biblical symbolism, the queen of a king is analogous to the city of a king, and the fact that the queen is pictured in Nehemiah 2:6 is part of the theology of the book of Nehemiah, which concerns rebuilding the Holy City.

The Persian Kings in Ezra 4–6

The only other matter to notice regarding Darius-Ahasuerus-Artaxerxes is this: he seems very concerned to favor the Jews. Every time he appears, he is favorable to them. In Esther he is tricked into harming them, but in Esther, the Jews deserve the threat that is issued against them. It seems that Darius was a great champion of "Zoroastrianism," having been taught by Zoroaster himself according to some authorities. Zoroaster's teaching is in so many respects similar to Judaism that it almost certainly demonstrates the influence of some devout Jew upon Zoroaster in the formation of his beliefs. It centered on a revelation of God in fire, corresponding to the revelation of God in the fiery glory cloud and in the altar fire in the Old Testament. It featured a Satanic opponent to God, who is often said to be equal to the good God, but may not always have been so considered. While much of Zoroastrianism fell back into polytheism, authentic Zoroastrianism was severely monotheistic and creationist, and there were always those who held to the old, pure form of it. Interestingly, Zoroaster's own poems speak of God (Ahuramazda) and His attributes, Good Word, and Holy Spirit! The magi who visited Jesus at His birth were Persians and almost certainly were faithful God-fearers. Thus, everything indicates that Darius, and also Cyrus, was a true God-fearing Gentile. The religion of the Persian God-fearers came to be called Zoroastrianism, but we should not let the dualistic and polytheistic later forms of Zoroastrianism confuse us. There were faithful Persian God-fearers in Jesus' day, just as there were faithful Jews.

Even if I have been too kind to Zoroastrianism, the fact is that Darius hated the polytheists. He would have been disposed to favor the Jews, for they alone, except for the Zoroastrians, were monotheists. I am pretty sure that any Zoroastrian who read the Hebrew scriptures would think they were saying the same thing he believed.

Six
The Seventy "Weeks" of Daniel 9:24–27

The assumption that the Artaxerxes of Ezra-Nehemiah was Artaxerxes Longimanus has caused many conservative Bible commentators to assume that the predicted decree to restore and rebuild Jerusalem (Dan. 9:25) refers to a decree issued during Longimanus's reign. In particular, the order given Ezra in the seventh year of "Artaxerxes" (Ezra 7:11ff.) is assumed to have been given in the seventh year of Longimanus, which was 457 BC. Adding a literal 490 years to that date we come to AD 33, and since the predicted crucifixion of the Messiah came in the middle of the 70th "week" (7) of years, we arrive at AD 30 for the death of Jesus Christ.

Attractive as this seems, there are two serious problems with it. First, it is quite clear that the decree to rebuild Jerusalem refers to the decree of Cyrus. The Bible prophesies that Cyrus would rebuild Jerusalem (Isa. 44:28; 45:1, 13). Right after Cyrus's decree, the rebuilding did begin (Hag. 1:2–4). Moreover, the whole point of Daniel 9 is that the 70 years of Jerusalem's captivity are ending.

Darius, Artaxerxes, and Ahasuerus in the Bible

That is the basis of Daniel's prayer. The answer to his prayer is that 70 "sevens" now lie ahead for the city. It is clear from the context that this new period of time takes up where the former period left off.

The second problem is that if the thesis of this monograph is correct, Artaxerxes Longimanus is not in the picture at all. The order given in Ezra 7 came from Darius, in his 7th year, which was 516/5 BC.

The short chronology of Ezra-Nehemiah does, however, shed light on Daniel 9:25. The 70 weeks are divided into a block of 7 and a block of 62 weeks, with one at the end. The text makes it clear that Jerusalem will be rebuilt during the block of 7 weeks and that the Messiah will be cut off after the block of 62 weeks, during the 70th.

Now as it turns out, 49 years from the decree of Cyrus takes us down to the end of Nehemiah.

539–531	Cyrus
530–523	Cambyses II
522–487	Darius–Artaxerxes

In terms of the 70 years of captivity, the year 539 was an "accession year" for Cyrus, whose reign by Jewish reckoning began in the fall of 538. There was trouble about granting release to the Jews, as we have seen from Daniel 10, and the decree did not come until 537, which was still part of Cyrus's first year by Jewish reckoning.

Counting forward 49 years, we come to 489, which is the 34th of Darius's 36 years. According to Nehemiah 13:6, Nehemiah returned to Artaxerxes (Darius) in the 32nd year of that king's reign. That was the year 491. Shortly thereafter Nehemiah returned to Jerusalem and set things right there. If we assume Nehemiah was away from Jerusalem for a year, we can

The Seventy "Weeks" of Daniel 9:24–27

easily see that he completed his work in the 34th year of Darius, in the 49th year of the prophesied period of time.

Since there are more than 490 years from the decree of Cyrus to 3 years after Jesus' crucifixion, the period must be symbolic. Since the last "week" is chronologically literal, since Jesus did minister for 3 1/2 years before being crucified in the middle of the "week," and since the first block of 7 "weeks" is a literal chronological 49 years, the symbolism is focused on the 62 sevens.

It is beyond the scope of this monograph to go into further detail here, so it will have to suffice to point out that the 70 years of captivity are typologically related to the 70 weeks that follow it until the coming of the Messiah. Daniel 5:31 tells us that Darius the Mede took over Babylon at about the age of 62. This is a very odd piece of information, because the age of no other Gentile king is ever given in the Bible. The effect of this information is to divide the 70 years of captivity into an initial 7 years, then the 62 years of Cyrus/Darius, and then a final year before the decree was issued. During that final year, as Daniel 6 records, Daniel was attacked, thrown into a den of lions, and then brought back. The typology is clear and has always been seen by Christian interpreters. Daniel's "death and resurrection" in the 7th year of the captivity is a type of Jesus' death and resurrection in the middle of the 7th week.

Chronological Appendix

Months begin in the spring. The first month is roughly April; the twelfth month is roughly March.

1J = year 1 by Jewish reckoning, which reckons king's years from autumn to autumn, beginning in the seventh month.

1P = year 1 by Persian reckoning, which reckons king's years from spring to spring, beginning in the first month.

539 BC

4th Quarter: Nabonidus flees Babylon, Belshazzar proclaims himself co-regent. The city falls. Ugbaru runs the city for 17 days, then turns it over to Cyrus/Darius, so that Darius the Mede "received" the kingdom. Eight days later Ugbaru, the governor, dies.[1] New governor is needed. Daniel is the most favored candidate. The events of Daniel 6. "The Accession year" of Cyrus (Darius the Mede), age 62, begins.

538 BC

2nd Quarter: Cyrus 1P (Persian). Cambyses II becomes co-regent with Cyrus of Babylon.

4th Quarter: Cyrus 1J. At the beginning of the quarter, Daniel's calculations lead him to the prayer of Daniel 9. At end of quarter, Cambyses II is removed as "king of Babylon," and Gabriel strengthens Cyrus (Daniel 11:1).[2] This is the beginning of the 70 weeks of years, and thus also of the 7 weeks of years.

---

1. William H. Shea, "Darius the Mede in his Persian–Babylonian Setting," *Andrews University Seminary Studies* 29:235-257. In this essay, Shea accepted and argued for identifying Darius with Cyrus. In a later essay, Shea reversed himself and has argued that Darius is Ugbaru and that Daniel served under him, not after him. I have not found this persuasive. But see Shea, "The Search for Darius the Mede (Concluded), or, The Time of the Answer to Daniel's Prayer and the Date of the Death of Darius the Mede," *Journal of the Adventist Theological Society* 12 (2001), 97-105.

2. Idem.

537 BC

1st Quarter: Cyrus, having removed Cambyses II, who opposed the Jews, decrees that the Jews are to rebuild the Temple.

2nd Quarter: The Jews travel to Palestine.

3rd Quarter: The Jews settle in.

4th Quarter: Cyrus 2J. The Feast of Tabernacles celebrated (Ezra 3), but the foundations of Temple are not yet laid. This begins the "second year of their coming to Jerusalem," Ezra 3:8.

536 BC

2nd Quarter: Work is begun on Temple in the second month, Ezra 3:8.

4th Quarter: Cyrus 3J. Opposition to rebuilding project arises, Ezra 4:1–3.

535 BC

1st Quarter: Opposition discourages the Jews from working on the Temple. Adversaries at Cyrus's court begin to frustrate the position of the Jews and Daniel, Ezra 3:4–5.

2nd Quarter:
  1st month, 4th day: Apparently Cambyses II became co-regent with Cyrus and stood against the Jews.[3]
  1st month, 24th day: God appears to Daniel after he mourns 3 weeks, because of the opposition to Temple building, Daniel 10:1–4.

4th Quarter: Cyrus 4J.

530 BC

4th Quarter: Cambyses II 1J. This begins the 9th year of the 70 weeks.

522 BC

3rd Quarter: In July, Pseudo-Smerdis seizes the throne. Cambyses II, on his way back from Egypt, dies, possibly by suicide. On September 29, Darius overthrows him and takes the throne.

4th Quarter: Darius 1J. This begins the 17th year of the 70 weeks. The Persian Empire is in turmoil, and Darius must reconquer almost all of it.

---

3. Idem.

521 BC

2nd Quarter: Darius 1P.

3rd Quarter:
> 6th month, last day: End of 70 years of God's desolation of the Temple.

4th Quarter: Darius 2J. Beginning of 18th year of 70 weeks. By the end of this year, Darius has reconquered most of the empire.

520 BC

2nd Quarter: Darius 2P. Haggai and Zechariah, possibly because their books deal with the rebuilding of the Temple, use the religious calendar and date Darius's reign from spring to spring.

3rd Quarter:
> 6th month, 1st day: Haggai rebukes the Jews for letting a year go by without rebuilding the Temple, Haggai 1:1.

4th Quarter: Darius 3J. Beginning of 19th year of 70 weeks.
> 7th month, 21st day: God promises to glorify the Temple, Haggai 2:1–9.
>
> 8th month: Zechariah calls on the Jews to repent, Zechariah 1:1–6.
>
> 9th month, 24th day: Haggai prophesies because the Temple foundation has been laid anew, Haggai 2:10, 18, 20.

519 BC

1st Quarter:
> 10th month, 10th day: 70th anniversary of the initial investiture of the Temple, when the cities of Judah were distressed by Nebuchadnezzar's army.
>
> 11th month, 24th day: Beginning 3rd or "resurrection" month after the Temple foundation was relaid. Zechariah mentions that the cities of Judah have been distressed 70 years (Zech. 1:12), and sees God cleanse the Temple and renew the covenant. Zechariah 1:6–6:8.

2nd Quarter: Darius 3P. Possibly in connection with New Year festivities, Darius/Ahasuerus begins a 6-month festival, Esther 1:3–4.

4th Quarter: Darius 4J. Beginning of 20th year of 70 weeks.
> 7th month (?): Darius/Ahasuerus gives a 7-day feast for everyone in Susa, Esther 1:5. Shortly thereafter, Vashti is deposed as senior queen.

518 BC— Darius campaigns in Egypt.
> *2nd Quarter:* Darius 4P
> *4th Quarter:* Darius 5J. Year 21 of the 70 weeks begins.
>> 9th month, 4th day: Zechariah answers questions about fasting, Zechariah 7:1. This is in the 71st year after the investiture of Jerusalem.

517 BC
> *2nd Quarter:* Darius 5P.
> *3rd Quarter:* 70th anniversary the burning of the Temple.
> *4th Quarter:* Darius 6J. Year 22 of 70 weeks begins.

516 BC
> *1st Quarter:* Esther is selected for trial as queen, Esther 2:12.
>> 12th month, 3rd day: The Temple completed, Ezra 6:15. This is in the 71st year after the fall of Jerusalem and the burning of the Temple.
>
> *2nd Quarter:* Darius 6P.
> *4th Quarter:* Darius 7J. Year 23 of 70 weeks begins.

515 BC—Darius campaigns in India.
> *1st Quarter:*
>> 10th month: Esther becomes queen, Esther 2:16.
>
> *2nd Quarter:* Darius 7P.
>> 1st month, 1st day: Ezra prepares to depart for Jerusalem, Ezra 7:8–9.
>> 1st month, 9th day: Ezra and his people gather at the river to depart, Ezra 8:15.
>> 1st month, 12th day: Ezra departs for Jerusalem, Ezra 8:31.
>
> *3rd Quarter:*
>> 5th month, 1st day: Ezra arrives in Jerusalem, Ezra 7:8–9.
>> 5th month, 4th day: Ezra's gifts were given in Jerusalem, Ezra 8:32–33.
>
> *4th Quarter:* Darius 8J. Year 24 of 70 weeks begins.
>> 9th month, 17th day: Ezra calls the people to assemble, Ezra 10:8.
>> 9th month, 20th day: The assembly under Ezra, Ezra 10:9.
>> 10th month, 1st day: Courts convene to assess marriages, Ezra 10:16.

514 BC

> *2nd Quarter:* Darius 8P.
>> 1st month, 1st day: The assessments of marriages concluded, Ezra 10:17.
>
> *4th Quarter:* Darius 9J. Year 25 of 70 weeks begins.

510 BC

> *2nd Quarter:* Darius 12P.
>> 1st month: Darius promotes Haman. Mordecai refuses to acknowledge the King's decree. Haman casts lots. Decree issued to exterminate Jews, Esther 3.
>>
>> 2nd month, 18th or 19th day: The last time Esther had visited Darius, Esther 4:11.
>>
>> 3rd month, 20th day: Mordecai reports the bad news to Esther. Esther's fast, Esther 4:16; 5:1.
>>
>> 3rd month, 22nd day: Esther's first feast, Esther 5:4, 8.
>>
>> 3rd month, 23rd day: Esther's second feast. Haman condemned. Darius issues decree that the Jews may defend themselves, Esther 8:9.
>
> *4th Quarter:* Darius 13J. Year 29 of 70 weeks begins.

509 BC

> *1st Quarter:*
>> 12th month, 13–14 days: The Jews defend themselves, Esther 9.
>>
>> 12th month, 14–15 days: The Jews rest and rejoice, Esther 9:17–18.
>
> *2nd Quarter:* Darius 13P.
>
> *4th Quarter:* Darius 14J. Year 30 of 70 weeks begins.

503 BC

> *2nd Quarter:* Darius 19P.
>
> *4th Quarter:* Darius 20J. Year 36 of 70 weeks begins.
>> 9th month: Nehemiah hears of the distress of Jerusalem, Nehemiah 1:1.

502 BC

> *2nd Quarter:* Darius 20P.
>> 1st month: Nehemiah is given permission to go to Jerusalem, Nehemiah 2:1.
>
> *3rd Quarter:*
>> 4th month, end: Nehemiah arrives in Jerusalem, Nehemiah 2:11.

> 5th month, beginning: Wall restoration is begun, Nehemiah 6:15.
>
> 6th month, day 25: Wall restoration is completed after 52 days.

4th Quarter: Darius 21J. Year 37 of 70 weeks begins.

> 7th month, day 1: The Feast of Trumpets. Covenant renewal at the Water Gate, Nehemiah 8:1.
>
> 7th month, day 2: Ezra's Bible study, Nehemiah 8:13.
>
> 7th month, days 15–22: The Feast of Tabernacles, Nehemiah 8:18.
>
> 7th month, day 24: Day of fasting and prayer, Nehemiah 9:1.

491 BC

4th Quarter: Darius 32J. Year 48 of 70 weeks begins. Some time in this year, Nehemiah returns to Darius, Nehemiah 13:6.

490 BC

2nd Quarter: Darius 32P.

4th Quarter: Darius 33J. Year 49 of 70 weeks begins. Nehemiah is away. On the basis of the wording of Nehemiah 13:30–31, I place Nehemiah's return to Jerusalem in this year, during 489 BC, completing the first 7 weeks and completing the rebuilding of spiritual Jerusalem.

www.ingramcontent.com/pod-product-compliance
Lightning Source LLC
Chambersburg PA
CBHW050606300426
44112CB00013B/2099